About the play

The People

- Oedipus, King of Thebes
- Jocasta, his wife
- Creon, Jocasta's brother
- Teiresias, a blind old wise man
- A messenger from Corinth
- An old servant
- Citizens of Thebes

How to say the names

Oedipus – Ee-di-pus
Jocasta – Joc-asta
Creon – Cree-on
Teiresias – Tie-ree-see-as

King Oedipus

Before this story begins,
Oedipus travelled from his own city
of Corinth to Thebes.
He found that Thebes had problems.
There was no King –
he had been killed
while travelling on a lonely road.
Also, the city was in the grip
of a monster, the Sphinx.
The Sphinx killed everyone
who couldn't answer her riddles.
Oedipus answered her riddle
and rid the city of her.
He was made King of Thebes.
He married the widow
of the old King, Jocasta.

But Thebes has fallen
on hard times again.

The Author

Sophocles *lived in Greece about 2500 years ago.*
He wrote many plays,
of which seven survive today.
He died in 406 BC at the age of 90.

LIVEWIRE
MYTHS AND
LEGENDS

SOPHOCLES'

King Oedipus

re-told by
Brandon Robshaw

Published in association with
The Basic Skills Agency

Hodder & Stoughton

A MEMBER OF THE HODDER

Acknowledgements
Cover: Fred van Deelen
Illustrations: Mike Bell

Orders; please contact Bookpoint Ltd, 39 Milton Park, Abingdon, Oxon OX14 4TD. Telephone: (44) 01235 400414, Fax: (44) 01235 400454. Lines are open from 9.00–6.00, Monday to Saturday, with a 24 hour message answering service. Email address: orders@bookpoint.co.uk

British Library Cataloguing in Publication Data
A catalogue record for this title is available from the British Library

ISBN 0 340 77513 0

First published 2000
Impression number   10 9 8 7 6 5 4 3 2 1
Year   2005 2004 2003 2002 2001 2000

Copyright © 2000 Brandon Robshaw

Typeset by GreenGate Publishing Services, Tonbridge, Kent.
Printed in Great Britain for Hodder and Stoughton Educational, a division of Hodder Headline Plc, 338 Euston Road, London NW1 3BH, by Atheneum Press, Gateshead, Tyne & Wear

Act One

Outside the Royal Palace at Thebes.
A crowd of citizens is waiting
for King Oedipus to come out.
They look hungry and thin.

Citizen 1   This is terrible.

Citizen 2   The King will help us.

Citizen 1   He'd better.

Citizen 2   He helped us before.
When he got rid of the Sphinx.

Citizen 1   But this is worse. Our crops have
failed. Our children are dying of
hunger. There's disease in the city.
Soon we'll all be dead!

Citizen 2   Don't worry. The King will do something.

Citizen 1   But what? What's he going to do?

Citizen 2   Here he comes now. We'll find out.

King Oedipus comes out
and stands on the palace steps.
He is wearing his royal robes.

Oedipus   My people!

Citizen 2   King Oedipus! Save us! Save our city!

Oedipus   I intend to. I know what
you are suffering.

Citizen 1	Oh, do you?
	What are you doing about it, then?
Oedipus	I am working to find out the cause
	of our problems.
	This hunger, this disease – it must
	all be a punishment.
	A punishment from the gods.
Citizen 1	A punishment? What for?
	I haven't done anything wrong!
Citizen 2	Ssh! Just listen.
Oedipus	I do not know what we have done
	wrong. But I intend to find out.
	And to put it right.
Citizen 1	How are you going to find out, then?
Oedipus	I have sent my brother-in-law, Creon,
	to the temple of Apollo. He will
	ask the priest what we must do.
Citizen 1	Where is he, then?
Oedipus	Here he comes now.

Enter Creon.

Oedipus	Creon! What did the priest say?
	Is it good news?
Creon	It could be. If we do what we should.
Oedipus	Tell us, then. What must we do?
Creon	Do you want me to speak
	in front of everyone?
Oedipus	Of course. These are my people.
	I have no secrets from them.
Creon	Well, then, the priest said that we
	are sheltering someone unclean here.
	A killer. A murderer.
	That is why the gods are punishing
	us. We must find the killer and
	drive him out. Then our city will
	return to good health.
	Our crops will grow again.
Oedipus	A killer? Whom did he kill?
Creon	Our last King. King Laius.
	He was killed while travelling on a
	lonely road.
Oedipus	And his killer is hiding here?
	Well, we shall find him.
	My people! You hear what Creon
	has said. If the killer is among you,
	let him give himself up!
	There is silence.

Oedipus   I promise that he will not be put to
              death. He will not be put in prison.
              He will have to leave the city,
              that is all.

Silence again.

Oedipus   It will be better for the killer if he
              gives himself up now.
              If, after this, I find the killer,
              he shall be blinded.
              Do you hear? Blinded!
              I shall put out his eyes!

Silence again.

Oedipus   Very well. You have been warned.
              I am going to find the killer.
              I shall avenge the death of King
              Laius as if he were my own father!

Citizen 2 King Oedipus! I have an idea.

Oedipus   Speak. I am listening.

Citizen 2 Why don't we ask old blind Teiresias?
              They say he has second sight.
              He may know who the killer is.

Oedipus   I have already sent for him.
              It was Creon's idea. He is on his way.

Creon   Look – here he comes now.

Enter Teiresias, being led by a servant.
He is old and blind.

5

Act Two

Oedipus	Welcome, Teiresias. We need your help. Though you are blind, you see many things in your mind's eye. There is a killer hiding in Thebes. Can you tell us who it is?
Teiresias	I'm sorry. I can't help you.
Oedipus	You don't know? That's a great pity.
Teiresias	I know. But I cannot say.
Oedipus	If you know, you must tell us!
Teiresias	I am sorry. Let me go home.
Oedipus	(*Getting angry*) Go home? No, you shan't go home – not until you've told us what you know! For the sake of Thebes, you must tell us!
Teiresias	For your own sake, I must not.
Oedipus	(*Very angry now*) Do you know who I am? I am your King! I order you to tell us – who is the killer?
Teiresias	I will say no more.
Oedipus	Do you know what I think? I think you won't tell us because *you* did it!

	It's you! You are the killer!
Teiresias	(*Getting angry himself*)
	Is that what you think?
	Then hear this – it's you!

Pause.

Oedipus	What?
Teiresias	You heard what I said.
Oedipus	Say it again.
Teiresias	No, I don't want to.
Oedipus	Say it again!
Teiresias	All right, since you force me.
	You are the killer.
Oedipus	(*To the citizens*) You hear this?
	You hear how he speaks to the King?
	(*To Teiresias*) If you weren't a blind
	old man, I'd ... Wait a minute.
	A blind old man ... You couldn't
	have killed King Laius on your own.
	Someone must have helped you.
	Who was it? Was it Creon?
Creon	What?
Teiresias	Creon has nothing to do with this.
	I tell you again: you are the killer.
	And that's not all.
Oedipus	What? There's more, is there,
	you blind old madman?
	Come on, then. Let's hear it.

Teiresias	Your wife – do you know who she is?
Oedipus	Of course I know who my wife is,
	you blind old fool!
Teiresias	You'll feel sick when you find out.
Oedipus	That's enough! Get out!
	Get out of here!
	Or I'll kill you where you stand!
Teiresias	(*Going*) You are angry now.
	By the end of the day, you will wish
	you had never been born.
	(*Exit Teiresias.*)
Oedipus	(*Turning on Creon*)
	Did you put him up to this?
Creon	No! I'm as surprised as you are!
Oedipus	You expect me to believe that?
	You're plotting against me –
	trying to take my throne!
Creon	I'm not! Why would you think that?
Oedipus	It was your idea to bring
	that blind old madman here.
	And then he calls me a killer
	in front of all my people.
	You must have put him up to it.
	You're trying to get rid of me –
	so you can be King yourself!

Creon	I'm not, honestly!
	I don't want to be King!
Oedipus	That's good,
	because you won't get the chance!
	I'll have you put to death!

Jocasta comes out of the palace.
She is some years older than Oedipus,
but still beautiful.

Jocasta	What's all this noise?
	My husband and my brother
	shouting at each other?
	What's going on?
Creon	Your husband says I must be
	put to death.
Jocasta	What? Why?
Oedipus	He's plotting against me –
	saying I'm a killer!
Creon	I'm not – I never said that!
Jocasta	Oedipus, you must believe my
	brother.
Oedipus	Why? Why should I believe him?
Citizen 1	He is your friend!
Citizen 2	And you have no proof against him.
Citizen 1	You must trust your friend.

Oedipus	Well ... all right.
	Because my people ask it.
	I won't have you put to death, Creon.
	But I still don't trust you.
	Or like you. You'd better get out of
	my sight.
Creon	(*Going*) This is so unfair.
Jocasta	Now, then, what's been going on?
Oedipus	He said I killed King Laius.
Jocasta	My brother said that?
Oedipus	Well, he didn't say it himself.
	It was that blind old madman,
	Teiresias. But Creon must have
	put him up to it.
Jocasta	I'm sure he didn't.
	But I can see you are worried
	by what Teiresias said.
	Listen to me.
	I can put your mind at rest.
Oedipus	Can you?
Jocasta	Yes, if you calm down and listen
	to me.

Act Three

Jocasta	Listen, Oedipus.
	Don't take any notice of Teiresias.
	He hasn't got second sight.
	There's no such thing.
Oedipus	Isn't there?
Jocasta	No – and I can prove it.
Oedipus	How?
Jocasta	A long time ago, King Laius
	was told that he would be killed
	by his own child – his child
	and mine. And what happened?
	Laius was killed by robbers –
	not by his child. So you see,
	you can't believe everything you hear.
Oedipus	What about the child?
Jocasta	We got rid of it.
	Left it on a mountain to die
	when it was a little baby.
	So you see,
	the story didn't come true.
Oedipus	And your husband –
	where was he killed?
Jocasta	A long way from here. At a place
	where three roads meet.

Oedipus	(*Getting worried*) Three roads, you say? Where, exactly?
Jocasta	Oh, between here and Corinth.
Oedipus	And when was this?
Jocasta	A long time ago. Just before you came here, in fact.
Oedipus	(*Quietly*) Oh, God. Oh, my God.
Jocasta	What? What is it?
Oedipus	I've got a terrible feeling that – but no, no, it can't be true!
Jocasta	What is it? Tell me!
Oedipus	Listen, then.
	As you know, my parents are
	the King and Queen of Corinth.
	But when I was a young man,
	I heard a terrible story –
	that it was my fate to kill
	my father and marry my mother.
	So I left home – just ran away.
	I didn't want there to be
	any chance of this story coming true.

Jocasta	That was wise.
Oedipus	But on my travels, I came to a crossroads where three roads join. And there was an old man in a carriage , with some servants. He ordered me out of the way. We had a row. Then he tried to stab me with his sword. So I got my stick and cracked him on the head with it. He died. His servants came for me – I killed them too. Only one escaped.
Jocasta	So – you think ...
Oedipus	It must have been King Laius. I killed him.

14

Jocasta	No, that can't be right. His servant said he was killed by robbers.
Oedipus	By robbers? More than one?
Jocasta	Yes, a gang of them. So it can't have been you.
Oedipus	Is this servant still alive?
Jocasta	Yes. Shall I send for him?
Oedipus	Yes. let's get him here. If he can swear that it was a gang of robbers, I'm all right. If it was a gang, it wasn't me.

They go into the palace.

Citizen 1	What do you think?
Citizen 2	It can't have been him.
Citizen 1	I hope you're right.
Citizen 2	I just can't believe it. It would be too tragic.
Citizen 1	A lot of tragic things happen in this life.

Enter a messenger.

Messenger	Is King Oedipus there?
Citizen 2	He's in the palace.
Citizen 1	Why do you want him?
Messenger	I have some news for him.

Act Four

Oedipus comes out of the palace with Jocasta.

Oedipus   I heard there was a messenger
with news for me.

Messenger   Yes – I have news for you
from Corinth.

Oedipus   Oh, yes? What's the news?

Messenger   The King of Corinth is dead.

Jocasta   What, Oedipus's father?

Messenger   Yes. You'll be made
King of Corinth now, Oedipus.

Jocasta   You hear that, Oedipus?
All that rubbish about killing your
own father – he's died on his own,
without your help!

Oedipus   What did he die of?

Messenger   Old age.

Oedipus   Then I am safe – safe from the
curse! I won't kill my own father.

Jocasta   I told you so all along.
You can't believe these stories.

Oedipus   You were right.

Jocasta   Just forget it now.

Oedipus	But there's still
	the other part of the curse …
Jocasta	What – marrying your mother?
Oedipus	Yes.
Jocasta	Don't be silly.
	You're not going to marry
	your own mother by accident,
	are you?
Oedipus	I suppose not – but as long as
	she's alive, it worries me …
Messenger	Is this your fear?
	That if you come back to Corinth,
	you'll end up marrying your mother?
Oedipus	That's the curse I was told of.
Messenger	Then you can put your mind at rest.
Oedipus	Why?
Messenger	The Queen of Corinth
	isn't your mother.
Oedipus	What do you mean?
Messenger	She's not your mother. And the
	King wasn't your father, either.
Oedipus	But – they brought me up.
	Treated me like a son.
Messenger	They had no children of their own.
Oedipus	So – how did they get me?
Messenger	You were found on a mountain
	when you were a baby.

17

Oedipus   Who found me? You?

Messenger   No, it was a servant of King Laius.
I met him by chance
and he gave you to me to look after.
I took you to the King and Queen
of Corinth. And they adopted you.

Oedipus   This servant who found me –
who was he?

Citizen 1   I think it's the man you've sent for.

Citizen 2   The one who saw King Laius
being killed by the robbers.

Oedipus   Isn't that strange? This same man
who clears me of the crime,
may tell me the secret of my birth.

Jocasta	(*Scared*) What do you want
	to know that for? Who cares?
	You're here now, aren't you?
	What does it matter
	how you were born?
Oedipus	It matters to me. I want to know
	who my parents were.
Jocasta	Why? Why not just leave it?
	What good can it do?
Oedipus	Why are you so worried?
	It can't do you any harm.
Jocasta	Just leave it, Oedipus.
Oedipus	I see. I get it now.
	You're worried my parents
	were slaves, is that it?
	You're a queen
	and you don't want to be married
	to a man of low birth.
Jocasta	I'm telling you for your own good.
	Leave it. Please. Or you'll be sorry.
Oedipus	I want to know the truth.
Jocasta	You fool!
	You'll be sorry you were ever born!
	Those are the last words I will say
	to you.

She runs into the palace.

Citizen 1	What's up with her?
Citizen 2	She seems scared.
Citizen 1	As if she has understood something terrible.
Citizen 2	And she dare not say what it is.
Oedipus	Whatever the truth is, I want to know it. I am not afraid. I want to know who I am!

Enter King Laius's servant. He is an old man.

Oedipus	Here he is at last! Old man, we have some questions to ask you.
Servant	If I can help, I will.
Oedipus	(*Pointing to the messenger*) Do you know this man?
Servant	I don't think so. I don't remember.
Messenger	It was many years ago. You gave me a baby boy – asked me to take care of it.
Servant	(*Nervously*) What if I did?
Messenger	Here he is! That baby is now the King!

Servant	Oh no – that must be a mistake.
Oedipus	Old man, you'd better be straight with us. I want the truth. *(He grips the servant by the arms)* The truth, now. Did you give this man a baby to care for?
Servant	Yes, I did. And I wish I hadn't! But I hadn't the heart to leave him to die.
Oedipus	And whose child was he?
Servant	He was … King Laius's child.
Oedipus	What? A child he had with some servant girl?
Servant	No, he was … the queen's child. *There is a long pause.*
Oedipus	What?
Servant	They said there was a curse on the baby – that he would grow up to kill his father and marry his mother. So I was told to take him away. But I hadn't the heart to let him die. I gave him to this man.

Oedipus   And so – that baby – was me.
Then the curse – but wait a minute.
I didn't kill King Laius. You said
he was killed by a gang of robbers.

Servant   I was too ashamed to say it was just
one man. So I said it was a gang.
But there was only one man.

Oedipus   Then that man … was me.
I killed my father.
And – my mother –
Jocasta – my mother is my wife!

He runs into the palace.

Act Five

Citizen 2	Poor Oedipus! How terrible.
	King of Thebes one moment,
	and the next –
Citizen 1	I wonder what he'll do.
Citizen 2	And what will Jocasta do?
Citizen 1	It just shows –
	no one can be called happy.
	Not until they're dead.
	While you're alive, you never know
	what will happen to spoil it.

Creon comes out of the palace.

He looks very grave.

Citizen 1	Creon! What's happened?
Creon	Very sad things. Terrible things.
Citizen 2	It can't be worse
	than what's already happened.
Creon	Listen, then.
	Queen Jocasta is dead.
Citizen 1	How did she die?
Creon	She ran into the palace,
	crying and screaming.
	She locked herself in her room.

	We didn't know what to do.
	Then Oedipus ran in.
	He broke her door down.
	And saw her hanging there.
Citizen 2	She killed herself?
Creon	Yes. But there was worse to come.
	Her dress was pinned
	with a gold brooch.
	Oedipus snatched the brooch
	and stuck the pin into his eyes.
	Again and again.
	Blood ran down and soaked
	his beard.

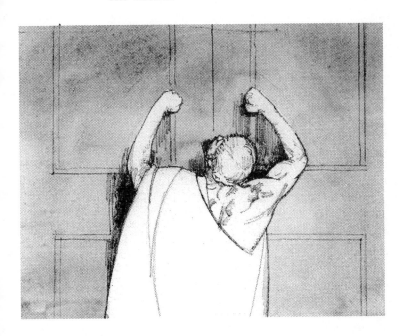

Oedipus comes out of the palace.
He is blind and gropes his way with his hands.
At the sight of him,
the citizens draw back in horror.
Some weep.

Oedipus   My people …

Citizen 1   King Oedipus – how could you do –
                such a terrible thing?

Oedipus   I swore the killer of King Laius
                should be blinded.
                And sent away.
                I must leave you now.
                I am your King no longer.

Citizen 2	Must you go?
Oedipus	I am the unclean thing –
	I am the reason this city was cursed.
	I killed my father. I married my
	mother. I am not fit to stay here.
Creon	Where will you go?
Oedipus	It doesn't matter.
	I will end my days as a wanderer.
	A blind old wanderer.
	Creon will take charge of the city
	now. But before I go …
Creon	Yes?
Oedipus	I must say goodbye to my children.

His two daughters are brought
from the palace.
He hugs them.

Oedipus	My daughters – my sisters!
	When you are older, you will
	understand why I had to go.
	Creon – you will look after them.
Creon	I will.

Oedipus turns and walks away,
his hands stretched in front of him.
He walks down the dusty road
away from the palace
and disappears into the distance.